Cambridge **Discovery Education**™

► **INTERACTIVE READERS**

Series editor: Bob Hastings

SLOW MOTION
TAKING YOUR TIME

A1+

Karen Holmes

CAMBRIDGE UNIVERSITY PRESS
Cambridge, New York, Melbourne, Madrid, Cape Town,
Singapore, São Paulo, Delhi, Mexico City

Cambridge University Press
32 Avenue of the Americas, New York, NY 10013-2473, USA

www.cambridge.org
Information on this title: www.cambridge.org/9781107691292

First published 2014
Reprinted 2014

Printed in Hong Kong, China, by Golden Cup Printing Company Limited

A catalog record for this publication is available from the British Library.

Library of Congress Cataloging-in-Publication Data

Holmes, Karen.
  Slow motion : taking your time / Karen Holmes.
      pages cm. -- (Cambridge discovery interactive readers)
   ISBN 978-1-107-69129-2 (pbk. : alk. paper)
1. Slow life movement--Juvenile literature. 2. Slow food movement--Juvenile literature.
3. English language--Textbooks for foreign speakers. 4. Readers (Elementary) I. Title.

HN20.H65 2013
320.6--dc23

                                    2013018628

ISBN 978-1-107-69129-2

Additional resources for this publication at www.cambridge.org

Layout services, art direction, book design, and photo research: Q2ABillSMITH GROUP
Editorial services: Hyphen S.A.
Audio production: CityVox, New York
Video production: Q2ABillSMITH GROUP

Contents

Before You Read:
Get Ready!

Why do things move slowly? Is it only because they can't move fast? Read on to learn why it can be good to take your time.

Words to Know

Complete the sentences with the correct words.

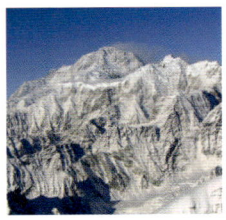

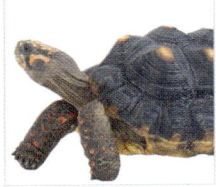

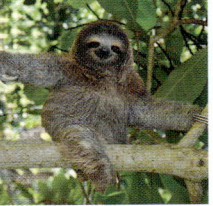

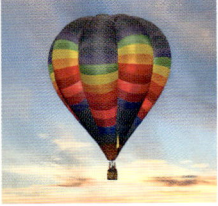

glacier

tortoise

sloth

hot air balloon

1. The ______________________ is the slowest animal in the world.
2. A ______________________ flies very slowly through the sky.
3. A ______________________ is a river of hard snow and ice.
4. A ______________________ has short legs and walks very slowly.

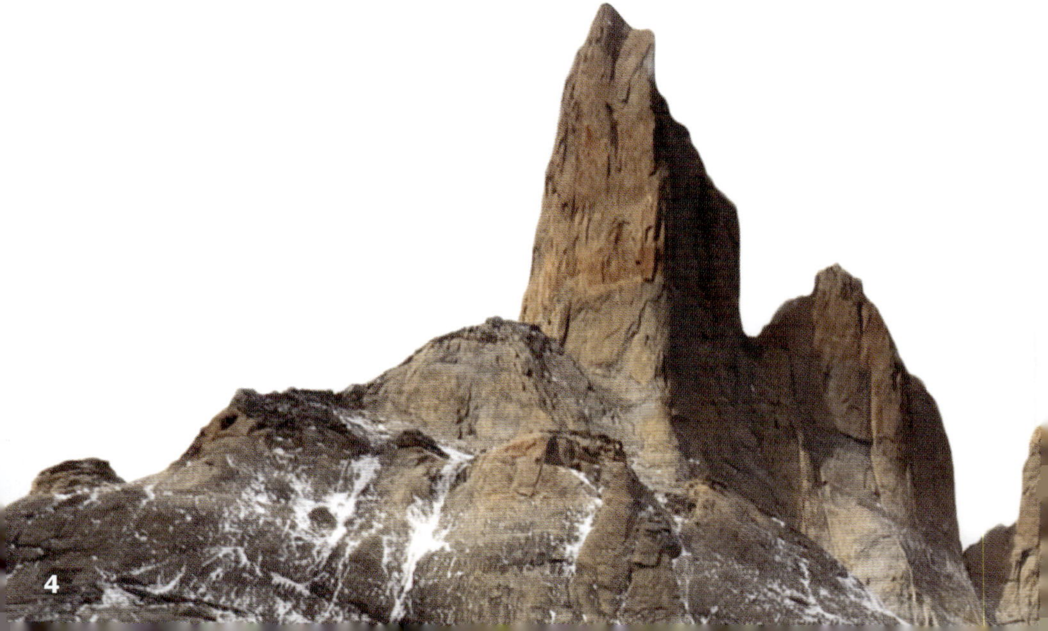

Read the paragraph. Then complete the definitions with the correct highlighted words.

Our world changes all the time but not everything moves quickly. In very cold places, the snow and ice between mountains slowly make glaciers. These glaciers go down the mountain like a river, but they move in slow motion. They are so slow you can't see them move. The land under our feet also changes because of the weather. These changes take one million or many millions of years. Living things can move slowly, too. Some trees grow very slowly, and some birds and animals need days to move from one place to another.

1 We live on the _____. We put houses and cities on it.

2 _____ are very high places. Everest is the highest.

3 A _____ is the word for 1,000,000.

4 When something _____, it goes from one place to a different place.

5 Boys usually _____ taller than girls.

6 Some cameras can take _____ videos.

Mountains are made of rock.

CHAPTER 1

What Moves Slowly?

ARE YOU BUSY TODAY? ARE YOU RUNNING FROM PLACE TO PLACE? ARE THERE FAST-MOVING CARS ON THE ROADS AND FAST-MOVING PLANES IN THE SKY?

Our world is **moving** and changing all the time. Some changes are very fast; for example, after a lot of rain a fast-moving river can **wash away** land. But not everything moves quickly. Some changes take millions of years. You can't see these slow changes – but they are happening every day, every week, every year.

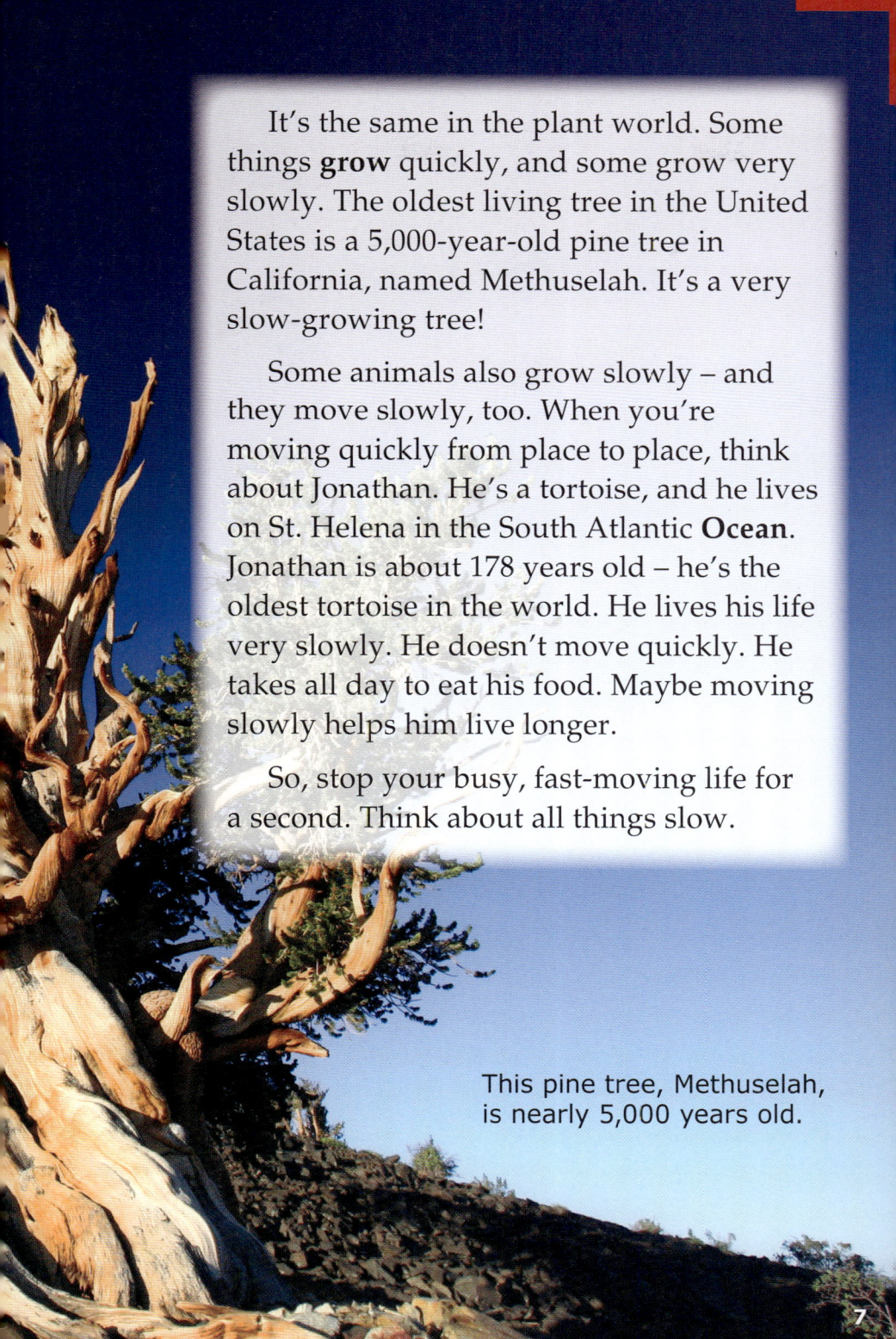

It's the same in the plant world. Some things **grow** quickly, and some grow very slowly. The oldest living tree in the United States is a 5,000-year-old pine tree in California, named Methuselah. It's a very slow-growing tree!

Some animals also grow slowly – and they move slowly, too. When you're moving quickly from place to place, think about Jonathan. He's a tortoise, and he lives on St. Helena in the South Atlantic **Ocean**. Jonathan is about 178 years old – he's the oldest tortoise in the world. He lives his life very slowly. He doesn't move quickly. He takes all day to eat his food. Maybe moving slowly helps him live longer.

So, stop your busy, fast-moving life for a second. Think about all things slow.

This pine tree, Methuselah, is nearly 5,000 years old.

CHAPTER 2

Slow Water

WATER CAN MOVE VERY QUICKLY. WE SEE IT RUNNING DOWN MOUNTAINS, IN RIVERS AFTER RAIN, AND IN THE OCEAN IN BAD WEATHER. BUT WATER CAN MOVE VERY SLOWLY, TOO.

When there are no mountains and the land is flat, the water in a river moves more slowly and gets warmer.

You can see this in the Everglades in Florida. The Everglades is the name of a large **piece** of land that is almost flat. In some places, there is some land above the water. In other places, the land is a little below the water. Water travels through the Everglades to the ocean very, very slowly.

Flat land

An alligator in the Everglades

The Everglades has hot weather and warm, slow water. So it is a good place to live for many different plants, animals, and birds. There are so many plants that some people call the Everglades the "River of Grass."

Alligators love the Everglades. These animals can swim in water and walk on land. They can find a lot of food here – fish, birds, and other animals. Alligators don't like people. They move away from them. But don't get too near to these big, strong animals and their long teeth. Or they may eat you!

Florida is very warm. The water there moves slowly – but it does move. Travel up to Alaska, and you're going to see very different slow-moving water. The water there moves slowly because it's ice!

There are more than 100,000 glaciers in Alaska. Many people think they are ice mountains. They're not – they are rivers of ice. This ice moves all the time. Most glaciers move about 0.3 **meters** a day but can move as fast as 31 meters in one day!

What makes these slow-moving glaciers? In cold weather, water comes down from the clouds as snow. The top layer[1] of snow is heavy. It makes the lower layers of snow into hard ice. Ice in high places slowly moves down to the ocean.

[1] **layer:** something flat between two other flat things; a cake sometimes has two or three layers.

This glacier in Alaska is a river of ice.

Some glaciers are so small you can walk over them in one or two hours. But others are very big. The biggest glacier in the world, the Lambert Glacier in Antarctica, is more than 40 kilometers wide and more than 400 kilometers long!

It's possible that one day soon the world is going to get warmer. Then the slow-moving glaciers are going to change into fast-moving rivers again.

Alaska and the Everglades are very different places. But they are both places where there is a lot of slow-moving water.

Video Quest

Glaciers

Watch the video about glaciers. What makes a glacier?

CHAPTER 3

Slow Land

IT'S NOT ONLY WATER THAT MOVES SLOWLY. THE LAND UNDER OUR FEET IS MOVING VERY SLOWLY, TOO.

Think about a mountain on a very wet and windy day. The wind and the water break small pieces from the rocks. These pieces move down the mountain. Maybe they **fall** into a river. Very, very slowly, they cover[2] the water, and the water goes under the land. The river becomes land. This is a big change – and it takes millions of years.

[2]**cover:** put one thing on top of another thing

Coal comes from trees and plants. We use coal to warm our homes.

Under the land, there are more changes. More than 300 million years ago, trees and plants covered a lot of the world. These trees and plants died, and the land covered them. Very slowly, the trees and plants changed into coal.

It takes a long time for the land to change. We can't see the mountains move. We can't see trees change into coal. But we can see things that move slowly in the plant and animal worlds.

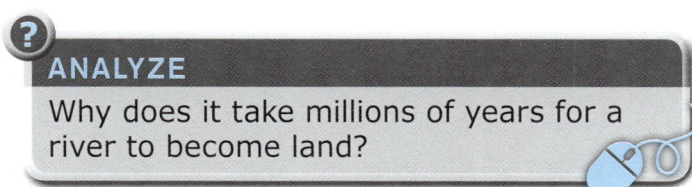

?

ANALYZE

Why does it take millions of years for a river to become land?

Look at the trees near you. Some grow very quickly, but others take hundreds of years to get big and tall. The world's slowest-growing tree is a White Cedar in Canada. After 155 years, it was only 10.2 cm tall! Interestingly, many slow-growing trees live longer than fast-growing trees.

It's the same for animals. Remember Jonathan the tortoise? Tortoises move slowly because they have heavy, hard shells on their backs and short, fat legs. They don't need to run away from other animals because these shells make them safe. And they don't need to move quickly to catch their food because they eat plants and other slow-moving animals.

A tortoise has a shell on its back.

White Cedar tree

The world's slowest animal is the sloth. Sloths live in trees and they sleep a lot – up to 20 hours a day. When they're not sleeping, they don't move much! They stay in trees and get most of their food and water from the plants and fruit near them. When they come down from the trees and want to go to another place, they move about two meters a minute – only 120 meters in an hour. We walk about five kilometers in an hour.

A sloth moves at about two meters a minute. People walk about five kilometers an hour.

So, not everything in the world wants to move fast!

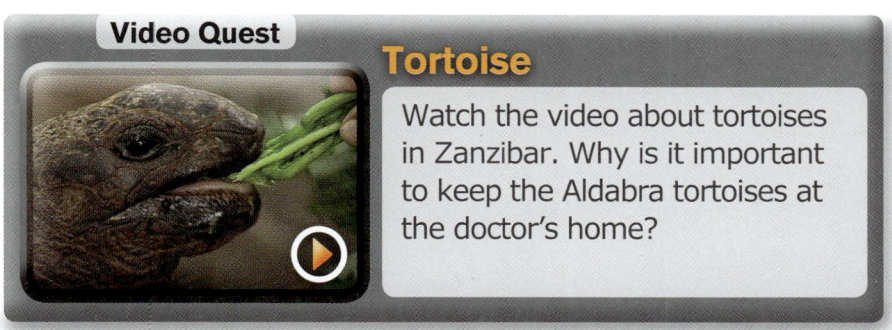

Video Quest

Tortoise

Watch the video about tortoises in Zanzibar. Why is it important to keep the Aldabra tortoises at the doctor's home?

CHAPTER 4

Slow Sky

WATCH A BIRD OR A PLANE FLY ABOVE YOUR HEAD. THEY MOVE VERY QUICKLY, DON'T THEY? BUT NOT ALL FLYING THINGS ARE SO FAST.

Every year, millions of people fly between cities and countries because a plane is much faster than a car or train. But some people don't want to fly quickly. They want to know the land below. To really see it, you need to fly slowly. You can't see much from a fast airplane high above the clouds. A hot air balloon is better! The wind moves these balloons. If the wind is not strong, they move very slowly through the sky.

Hot air balloons move slowly if there is little wind.

In France in 1783, brothers Jacques and Joseph Montgolfier were the first people to travel in a hot air balloon. In 1785, Jean Pierre Blanchard and an American, John Jeffries, flew from England to France in a hot air balloon. Their balloon started to go down into the ocean. They threw[3] everything heavy out of the balloon into the water below. But the balloon didn't go up. They took off their clothes and threw them into the water! The balloon moved up into the sky again.

It took them 2.5 hours to travel less than 40 kilometers. Now it only takes seven hours to fly from New York to London – and that's more than 5,500 kilometers!

....

[3] **throw:** send something through the air with your hands; past tense is "threw."

?

ANALYZE

Why did Blanchard and Jeffries throw things out of the balloon when it started to fall?

CHAPTER 5

Slow Motion

CAN WE MAKE THE WORLD GO SLOWER? CAN WE MAKE TIME GO SLOWER? NO, WE CAN'T. BUT WE CAN SEE THINGS MOVE MORE SLOWLY.

Lewis is a cameraman. He makes movies of sports people – runners and football players – in slow motion. This is how a slow-motion movie works. Lewis uses a **high-speed** camera to make a movie. When he watches the movie at normal speed, the runners and football players move very slowly.

Sports teachers use Lewis's slow-motion movies. They look at the runners moving their legs. They study the football players kicking the ball. They learn from the best players. Then they teach their students to be better at their sports.

Hockey players
with graphite sticks

Other people use slow-motion movies, too. For example, some hockey stick makers made movies of players using old wooden[4] sticks and new graphite[5] sticks. They watched the two movies in slow motion. This helped them to make new, better sticks.

Slow-motion movies don't really slow down the world. But they help us see it more closely – and we can learn a lot from them.

[4]**wooden:** made from wood; we get wood from trees.
[5]**graphite:** the hard, black part of pencils

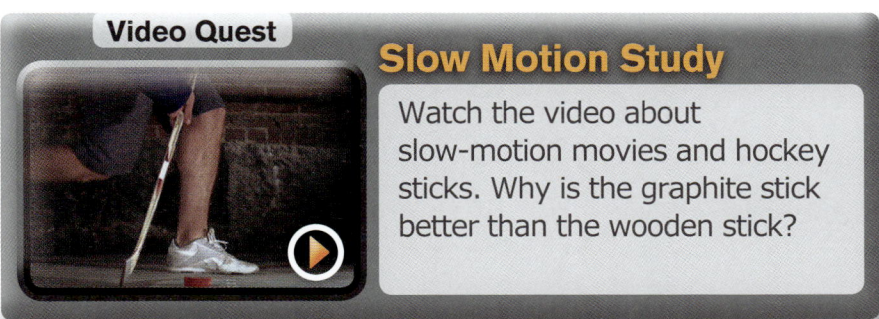

Video Quest

Slow Motion Study

Watch the video about slow-motion movies and hockey sticks. Why is the graphite stick better than the wooden stick?

CHAPTER 6

What Do You Think?

THINK ABOUT SOMETHING YOU DO SLOWLY, SOMETHING YOU ENJOY. WHY DO YOU LIKE TO DO THIS THING SLOWLY?

Some people think we live too fast. We don't have time to look at all the beautiful things in our world. We're too busy running from place to place.

In countries all over the world, people are learning to live more slowly. They don't drive cars; they ride bikes. They don't buy their fruit and vegetables in supermarkets; they grow them on land near their homes. They don't eat fast food; they cook at home.

People in the Slow Food Movement grow their food.

A small group of people in Italy started Slow Food in 1986. Now, there are 100,000 people in 150 Slow Food groups across the world. They help people learn about the land. They help them grow their food. They think that living more slowly is better for us.

Of course, we're all different. Living slowly isn't for everybody. Sometimes, we need to move quickly. But the world around us shows that fast and slow can live together.

Go fast or go slowly? What do you think?

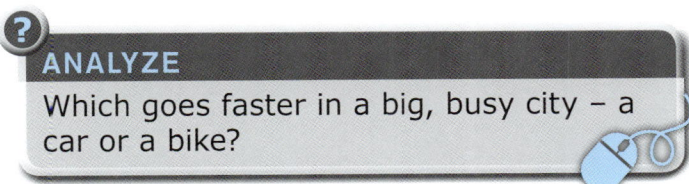

? ANALYZE

Which goes faster in a big, busy city – a car or a bike?

After You Read

Read the sentences and choose Ⓐ (True) or Ⓑ (False).

1 A tortoise moves faster than a sloth.

Ⓐ True
Ⓑ False

2 A glacier is made of rock.

Ⓐ True
Ⓑ False

3 Alaska is famous for the Everglades.

Ⓐ True
Ⓑ False

4 A glacier can move more than 25 meters in a day.

Ⓐ True
Ⓑ False

5 A sloth can move five kilometers in an hour.

Ⓐ True
Ⓑ False

6 A hot air balloon moves with the wind.

Ⓐ True
Ⓑ False

7 Some new hockey sticks are made with graphite.

Ⓐ True
Ⓑ False

8 People in Slow Food groups like fast-food restaurants.

Ⓐ True
Ⓑ False

Complete the Sentences

Use the words in the box to complete the sentences.

glacier   high-speed   moves   ocean   pieces

1. A sloth _____ slowly.
2. There is an _____ between the United States and the United Kingdom.
3. You can break something big into smaller _____.
4. A _____ train goes very quickly from one city to another.
5. A _____ is a river of hard snow and ice.

Answer the Questions

Answer the questions with full sentences.

1. Why is the Everglades called the "River of Grass"?

   _____

2. Which is the slowest-growing tree in the United States?

   _____

3. How many people are in Slow Food groups across the world?

   _____

Your Opinion

Talk or write about these questions.

1. What is one thing you do slowly?

   _____

2. Why do you do this thing slowly?

   _____

3. One day you may do this thing quickly. Are you going to enjoy it more, less, or the same?

   _____

Answer Key

Words to Know, page 4

1 sloth **2** hot air balloon **3** glacier **4** tortoise

Words to Know, page 5

1 land **2** Mountains **3** million **4** moves **5** grow
6 slow motion

Video Quest, page 11

Water running down mountains in very cold places.

Analyze, page 13

Small pieces of rock fall into rivers. Over a very long time
they cover the water, and the water goes under the land.

Video Quest, page 15

It is important that they stay there so they are safe.

Analyze, page 17

Blanchard and Jeffries threw things out of the balloon to
make it lighter so it would stay up in the sky.

Video Quest, page 19

You can play with a graphite stick for years longer.

Analyze, page 21   *Answers will vary.*

True or False?, page 22

1 A **2** B **3** B **4** A **5** B **6** A **7** A **8** B

Complete the Sentences, page 23

1 moves **2** ocean **3** pieces **4** high-speed **5** glacier

Answer the Questions, page 23

1 It is home to many plants. **2** The White Cedar is the
slowest. **3** There are 100,000 people in Slow Food groups.

Your Opinion, page 23   *Answers will vary.*